Main   Jan 2020

This item no longer
belongs to Davenport
Public Library

MARINE CORPS BASE
MASTER FILE
ENGINEERING FACILITIES

THE SCIENCE OF OPTICAL ILLUSIONS

DAVENPORT PUBLIC LIBRARY
321 MAIN STREET
DAVENPORT, IOWA 52801-1490

SEEING THINGS!

Gareth Stevens
PUBLISHING

ANNA CLAYBOURNE

Please visit our website, **www.garethstevens.com**.
For a free color catalog of all our high-quality books,
call toll free 1-800-542-2595 or fax 1-877-542-2596.

Cataloging-in-Publication Data
Names: Claybourne, Anna.
Title: Seeing things! / Anna Claybourne.
Description: New York : Gareth Stevens Publishing, 2020. | Series: The science of optical
illusions | Includes glossary and index.
Identifiers: ISBN 9781538242476 (pbk.) | ISBN 9781538241882 (library bound) | ISBN
9781538242483 (6 pack)
Subjects: LCSH: Optical illusions--Juvenile literature. | Visual perception--Juvenile literature.
Classification: LCC QP495.C5725 2020 | DDC 152.14'8--dc23

First Edition

Published in 2020 by
Gareth Stevens Publishing
111 East 14th Street, Suite 349
New York, NY 10003

Copyright © Arcturus Holdings Ltd, 2020

Photo credits: p22 Pere Borrell del Caso / Public Domain; p23 b DEA / G. DAGLI ORTI; p25
© Julian Beever; p29 br David Fleetham / Alamy Stock Photo

All rights reserved. No part of this book may be reproduced in any form
without permission from the publisher, except by a reviewer.

Printed in the United States of America

CPSIA compliance information: Batch #CS19GS: For further information contact Gareth Stevens, New York, New York at
1-800-542-2595.

CONTENTS

INTRODUCTION

WHAT ARE OPTICAL ILLUSIONS?

The word "optical" has to do with light and how we see it. An illusion is something that tricks you, so that you don't experience it as it really is.

Magicians and illusionists make impossible things appear to happen. This performer can't really make this die levitate—but he makes it look as if he can.

SEEING IS BELIEVING

When we look around and see things, it feels to us as if we're simply seeing the world as it really is. However, that's not quite true. Your eyes and your brain can make mistakes, miss things, or even see things that aren't there. An optical illusion is a picture that takes advantage of these mistakes to play a trick on you.

HOW HUMANS SEE

1. Light rays from objects enter the eye.

2. Light hits the retina at the back of the eyeball.

3. Light-sensitive cells in the retina detect patterns of light.

4. The cells send signals to the brain along the optic nerve.

5. The brain interprets the signals to figure out what they mean.

Retina   Image on retina

Eyeball

Visual cortex

Optic nerve   Brain

TOO MUCH INFORMATION!

All day long, there's a constant flood of images entering your eyes and zooming into your brain. There's so much information, your brain simply can't process it all carefully.

Instead, it decides what it's looking at by matching the light patterns it sees to its memories and previous experiences. It ignores or shuts out things that don't seem important and will quickly jump to conclusions to save time.

Here's an example. What can you see in this picture? ▶

Most people would see two friends riding these. ▼

In other words, bicycles—machines with two round wheels of equal size. But you only "see" that because of your brain's knowledge and experience. The wheels you actually saw look like this:

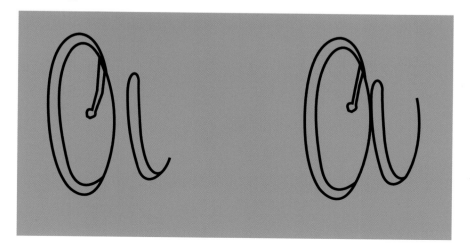

ILLUSIONS GALORE

This book is packed with incredible optical illusions to bamboozle your brain—from pictures that change color to shapes that vanish before your very eyes. Turn the page to get started!

5

AFTERIMAGES

Afterimages are what you see after you've looked at something. They're like weird, visual echoes!

For this illusion, you'll need a piece of plain white paper. Keep it ready nearby, then start staring at the woman's face below. Focus your eyes on the nose in the middle, and keep them there for about 30 seconds.

Now, look at your white paper. What do you see?

You should see a white face on a dark background, similar to a pirate flag. This effect is called an afterimage, and it's mainly caused by your eyeballs.

How Does It Work?

Inside the back of the eyeball is the retina—a layer of light-sensitive cells that detect light coming into the eye. If they see the exact same thing for a long time, the cells get "tired." They stop responding to the colors and become less sensitive to them.

When you look at the white paper, the cells are still less sensitive to the colors they were looking at, and more sensitive to the opposite colors. So, you see black where the image was white, and white where it was black.

The effect doesn't last long, but you should be able to see the afterimage for a few seconds.

The strange face afterimage illusion

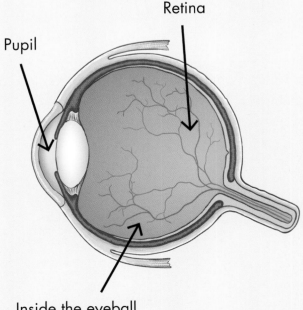

Retina

Pupil

Inside the eyeball

COLOR FLIP

Whatever color you stare at, you'll see the opposite in the afterimage—and that works with bright colors, too. For example, red is the opposite of green.

To test this, stare at Picture 1 for 30 seconds, then look at Picture 2. Picture 2 is actually black and white, but the afterimage makes you see the real colors.

Picture 1

Picture 2

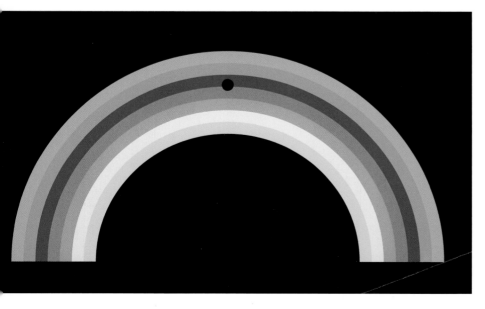

INSTANT RAINBOW

In this picture, all the colors are the opposite of what they should be. Stare at the dot for 30 seconds, then look up at the sky.

Ta-da—an instant rainbow!

AFTERIMAGE ADVENTURES

You can use afterimage illusions to create some amazing effects.

Stare at the plus sign on the green bird for 30 seconds without moving your eyes around. Then look straight at the cage. The bird is inside (and it's changed color, too!). It's the afterimage in your eyeballs that has made the bird appear.

REVERSE AFTERIMAGE

The next afterimage illusion works in a slightly different way. It's mainly yellow, so you might expect to see the opposite of yellow (purple) in the afterimage. But that's not what happens. Try it—stare at the black dot in the first picture for 30 seconds, and then look at the black dot in the second picture.

Instead of seeing the opposite color, the yellow and the white swap places. How does this work? No one is really sure!

The bird in cage illusion

The mysterious yellow dots illusion

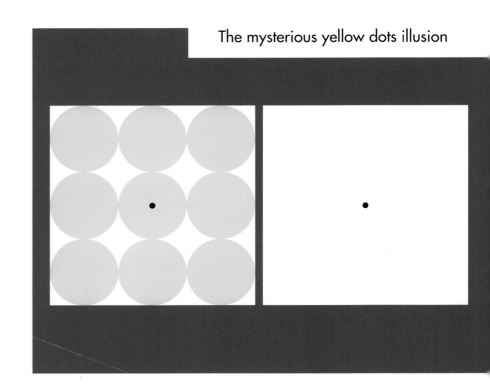

LEAKING AFTERIMAGE

Here's another variation. Stare at the first circle for 30 seconds, then look at the dot—you'll see a contrasting-colored afterimage.

Do the same with the second circle, and then look at the black ring. The afterimage color looks stronger and starts to "leak" out of the gap.

A leaking afterimage

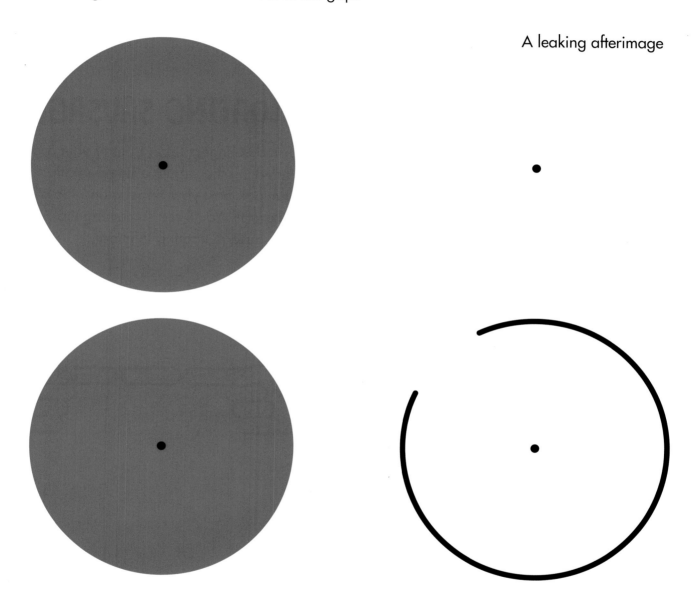

Brain-Boggling!

If this is how the retina works, why don't we see afterimages all the time? Well, we do see faint ones, but the brain mostly ignores them. They aren't very strong because normally, your eyes move around constantly and don't settle on one thing for long.

3-D THRILLS

Your eyes are constantly seeing the world from two different angles. This can be used to create strange effects.

Most people, unless they are visually impaired, see with two eyes. Although the eyes are close together, they are in slightly different positions. This means that they have slightly different views of the world and objects in it, which helps them to see in 3-D. But it can also cause some strange effects, such as the floating sausage illusion.

THE FLOATING SAUSAGE

Hold your index fingers up in front of your face, pointing at each other about a finger width apart. Then look past your fingers, and focus on the opposite wall. You'll see something that looks like a short sausage floating in midair.

The floating sausage illusion

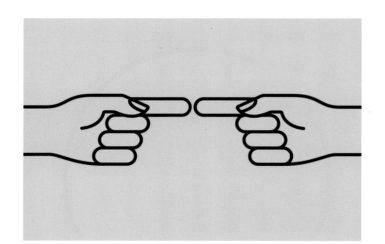 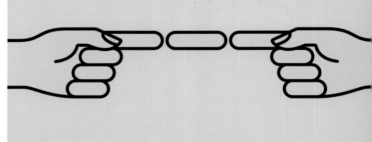

How Does It Work?

If you take turns closing your left and right eye, you'll see that each eye gives you a slightly different view of your fingers. From your left eye, they look farther to the right, and from your right eye, they look farther to the left. With your fingers in this position, the two views make your fingertips overlap, creating the "sausage."

You can't see it when you look straight at your fingers, because your eyes focus on them and turn the two views into a 3-D picture. But when you look into the distance, the sausage becomes visible.

10

HOLE IN YOUR HAND

For an even weirder experience, use the two views from your two eyes to see right through a large hole in your hand!

Take a cardboard paper towel tube (or roll up a sheet of paper), hold it in your left hand, and look through it with your left eye.

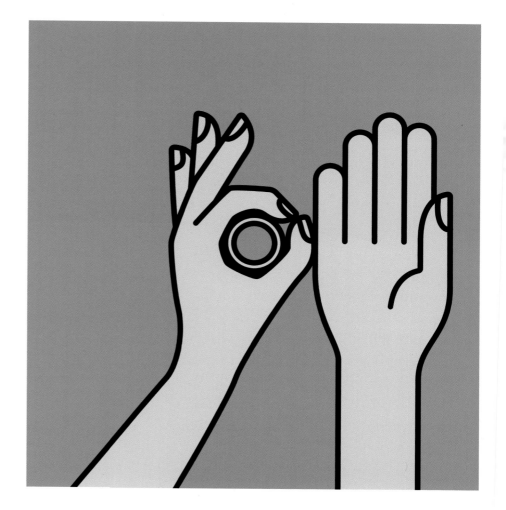

Horrible illusion: a hole in your hand

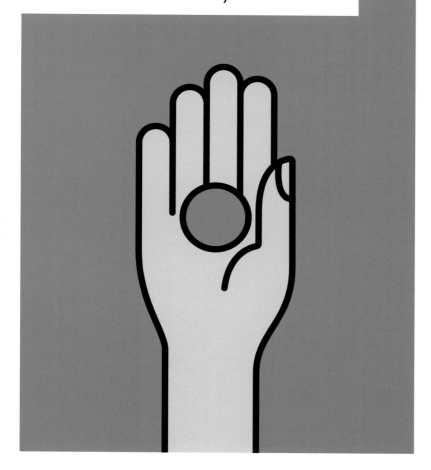

Hold your right hand next to the tube, and look at it with your right eye. Stare into the distance or at the other side of the room, the same as you did before. The hole in the tube will seem to merge with your hand, so it looks as if you can see right through it! When you look farther away, your eyes see both images separately—and then your brain combines them.

BLIND SPOT

Each of your eyeballs has a blind spot that sees nothing. Here's how to find it.

The retina at the back of the eye is covered in light-detecting cells—or almost covered. Each retina actually has a gap in it that lets the optic nerve—the bundle of fibers that carries light signals from the eye to the brain—through. So there's a part of each retina that doesn't see anything—the "blind spot." Yet, you hardly ever notice it!

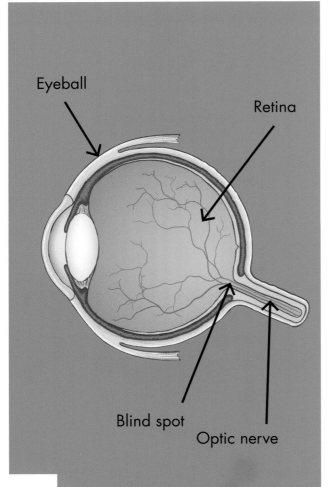

Eyeball

Retina

Blind spot

Optic nerve

FIND YOUR BLIND SPOT

To find your blind spot, hold this picture up in front of your face.

Cover your left eye, and look at the cross with your right eye.

Move the page slowly away from you, still looking at the cross.

When the cow passes into your right eye's blind spot, it will vanish.

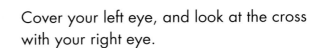

How Does It Work?

Normally, your two eyes "cover" each other's blind spots, so you never notice them. Even with only one eye open, your brain takes in information as you look around and uses it to "fill in" the blind spot. However, the trick above helps you find it by keeping your eye fixed at a sideways angle.

THE DISAPPEARING FINGER

Here's another amazing trick to find blind spots. Hold your hands up like this, with your index fingers sticking up, your thumbs touching, and your arms slightly bent.

Close your left eye, and stare at your left finger with your right eye. Now, wiggle your right finger from side to side.

Adjust the distance back and forth, and you should be able to make the wiggling finger disappear and reappear as it moves through your blind spot.

BLIND SPOT BACKGROUND

This test works just like the first one but has a background. Follow the the instructions from "Find Your Blind Spot" on page 12. When the X disappears, your brain "fills in" the background, so there's no gap.

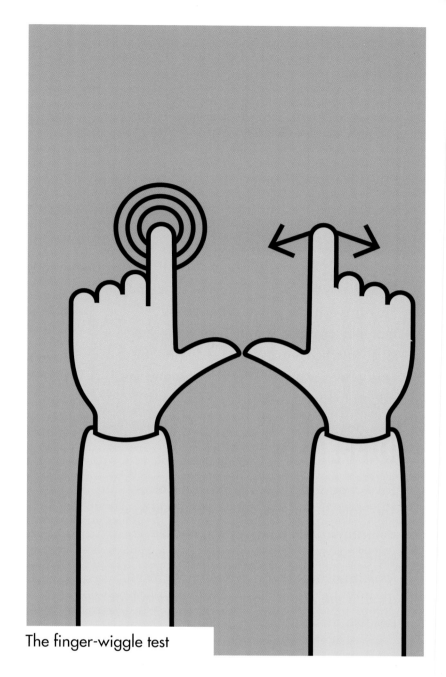

The finger-wiggle test

Blind-spot background test

CORNER OF MY EYE

Your eyeballs are round and don't have any corners. So what does "the corner of your eye" mean?

People say this when they see something they are not looking straight at, but that they glimpse somewhere off to the side. In other words, they see it in their "peripheral vision"—the part around the edge of what the eyes are looking at.

DIFFERENT DOTS

Take a good look at the picture below. The dots around the edge definitely look different from the dots in the middle, right? Now stare at the middle, and don't look anywhere else. You'll see the dots around the edge change and start to look just like those in the middle.

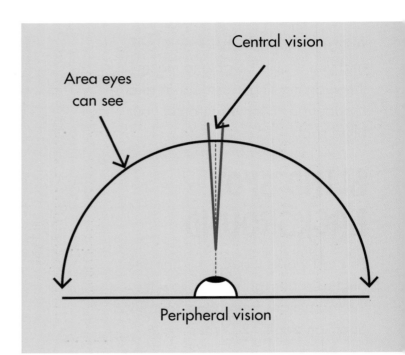

The different dots illusion

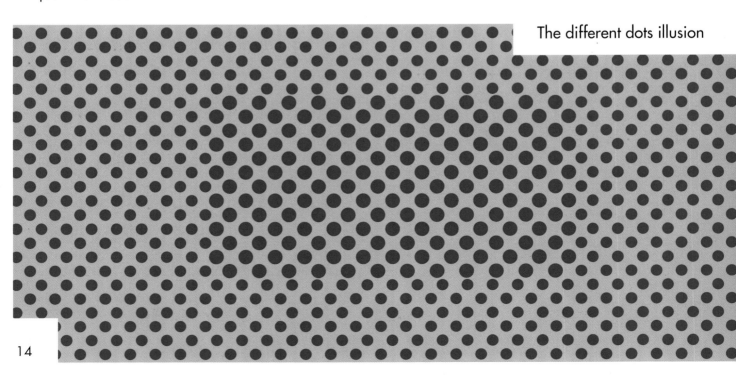

14

How Does It Work?

Your peripheral vision isn't very clear at all. In fact, it's fairly blurry and unclear! So, your brain helps out by filling it in with what it thinks should be there. With the illusion on page 14, it looks at the middle of the picture and decides it should all look like that!

On the right is another similar illusion to try. This time, stare at the dot in the middle.

Brain-Boggling!

Have you ever jumped out of your skin when you thought you saw a spooky figure out of the corner of your eye—only to discover it was just a coat on a hook or a harmless shadow? This can happen when your brain makes the wrong assumption about something in your peripheral vision.

Take this picture of a spooky room, for example. Look at it out of the corner of your eye, and you might notice some strangely spooky shapes. Look straight at it, and they're not quite so mysterious!

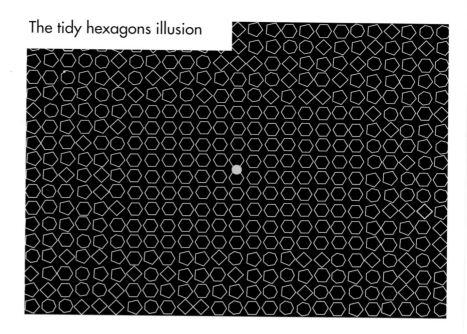

The tidy hexagons illusion

15

WHERE DID IT GO?

Now you see it—now you don't!

These illusions have parts that you can only see sometimes. No matter how hard you look, the things you're looking for keep disappearing!

MISSING DOTS

This grid illusion has 13 white dots in it. Yes, 13—count them! That's actually really difficult to do. The only way is to look at each cross in the grid, one by one, until you've checked them all off. And even if you do count all 13 dots, you still can't see them all at once. In fact, the most dots you can see at one time is probably only two or three.

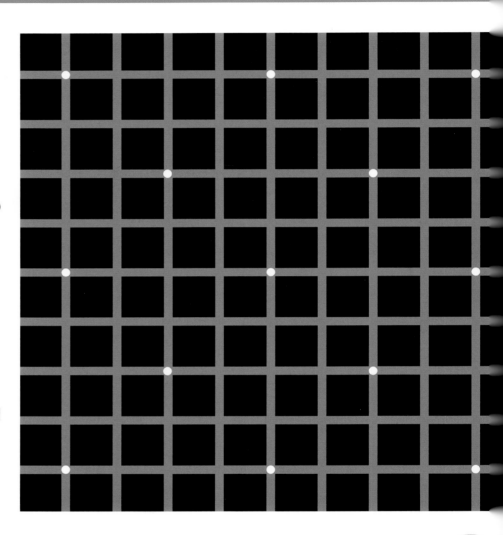

How Does It Work?

This type of illusion is called an "extinction" illusion—because parts of it seem to be going extinct all the time. Scientists think it works because of the way light sensors are packed together in your retina. Sometimes, especially if you are looking at a repeated pattern, each light sensor is influenced by the ones next to it.

This means that you can fail to see a dot that is really there, because your eyes are confused by the other patterns nearby—the crosses with no dots.

The scintillating dots extinction illusion

DIAGONAL DOTS

Above is another famous extinction illusion to try. This time, see if you really can count the dots yourself.

Brain-Boggling!

Want to see something else disappear? Would you believe you can make the blue rectangles in this picture completely vanish?

Just stare at the black dot, and don't move your eyes. Keep looking—don't give up. Then, after you've been looking for about 20 to 30 seconds—they're gone!

17

IMAGINARY SHAPES

Give your brain half a chance, and it will see all kinds of things that aren't there.

What can you see on these pages? Triangles, a square, a ball, and even some animals? Actually, they aren't really there. Yet again, it's your creative brain that likes to "fill in the gaps."

KANIZSA TRIANGLE

The most famous example of this is the Kanizsa triangle. It was created by Gaetano Kanizsa, an Italian scientist and artist, in 1955. Take a good look at it!

The picture is made up of just three dots with wedges cut out of them and three bent lines. Yet, you can't help "seeing" a solid yellow triangle.

On top of this, the yellow triangle actually seems to look brighter than its background, so you can see its edges all the way around! Here are two more examples to try. ▼

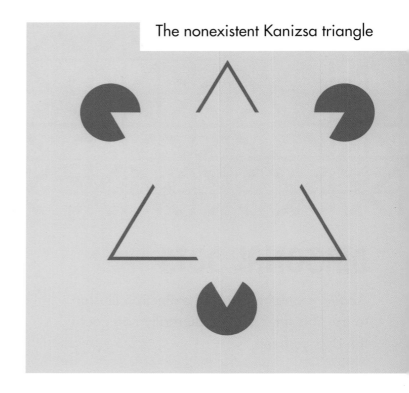
The nonexistent Kanizsa triangle

How Does It Work?

In everyday life, your brain has to figure out what objects are, even though they might be halfway hidden. So, for example, if you see someone standing in a doorway with their left side hidden, you don't think, "Ugh! This person's been chopped in half!" Your brain just identifies the whole shape from the parts you can see.

You do this all the time without thinking about it. The Kanizsa shapes simply highlight this brain behavior and put it to the test.

KANIZSA CREATURES

The same effect can even make you see a 3-D shape, such as this "ball." ▶

And what do the shapes below make you think of? Again, your brain doesn't just see what it sees—it collects clues and quickly leaps to conclusions. ▼

The spiky ball illusion

Is there something behind this tree?

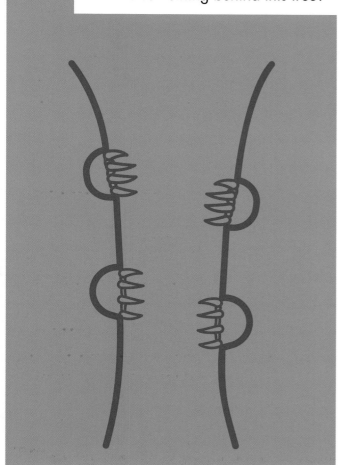

Instead of parts of a monster, you see a whole monster that's half submerged.

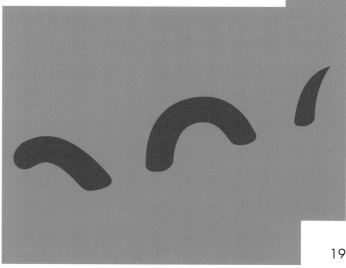

FACE FOOLERS

This picture of a famous face is upside down—but otherwise, it looks pretty normal ... doesn't it?

Try turning the book upside down, so you can see the face the right way up!

You'll soon see that the face isn't normal at all. Its eyes and mouth are flipped the wrong way, giving it a strange, monstrous look. But when the face is upside down, we hardly notice.

How Does It Work?

A face is one of the most important things your brain can see. We are hardwired to look very carefully at other people's faces, so that we can figure out how they are feeling toward us.

Normally, you take in the whole face shape and the arrangement of the features. When the face is upside down, it's harder to do that. Instead, your brain looks at the individual parts. If the eyes look OK, the mouth looks OK, and so on, your brain is happy.

But turn the altered face the right way up again, and your brain goes back to looking at the overall effect. Suddenly, you notice that something is very wrong!

The upside-down face illusion

TRY IT YOURSELF

To create this illusion using your own face, print out two copies of a clear, forward-facing portrait of yourself. Cut out the eyes and mouth from one, and glue them onto the other one upside down. Turn it upside down, and try it out on your friends and family!

Brain-Boggling!

In both these pictures, the eyes are exactly the same. But in one picture, they're looking at you, and in the other, they're to the side! We take cues from the shape and angle of the face to figure out who or what others are looking at.

TROMPE L'OEIL
Trick your eye with these very clever illusions.

"Trompe l'oeil" is French for "trick the eye." It's a type of painting or other art that tricks you into thinking you're looking at something 3-D when it's actually not 3-D at all. You can find trompe l'oeil effects in paintings and murals dating back to ancient times.

ESCAPE FROM THE FRAME

This amazing example is a painting by illusion-loving nineteenth-century artist Pere Borrell del Caso. It's called *Escaping Criticism* and shows a boy who seems to be climbing right out of the painting he's in. ▼

Pere Borrell del Caso's *Escaping Criticism*, from the year 1874.

How Does It Work?

To create a successful trompe l'oeil picture, you have to be able to paint or draw very realistically and be good at using perspective to make things look 3-D. But that's not all there is to it. After all, many paintings are well-painted and look 3-D. True trompe l'oeil also shows something that could really be happening, or existing, in the place where the picture is—and at the same scale.

In *Escaping Criticism*, for example, the boy is life-size, so he looks exactly as he would if a real boy climbed out of the wall. The painter also uses a trick frame to add to the effect—it's actually part of the painting!

The mind-bending *Mur des Canuts* in Lyon, France

ILLUSION STREET

Trompe l'oeil also works brilliantly on buildings. This amazing mural in France is on a flat wall, but it looks like a city scene—with trick steps, buildings, people, and stores. ▲

ON THE STAGE

Trompe l'oeil illusions are also useful in the theater, where they are used to make convincing stage sets. Viewed from the audience, they can create a convincing city, courtyard, or landscape. ▶

A painted trompe l'oeil theater backdrop

SIDEWALK PICTURES

With just some chalk, sidewalk artists can create 3-D worlds, visions, and monsters.

This mind-boggling sight looks like a series of waterfalls plunging into a chasm in the ground. In fact, it's just a chalk drawing on a sidewalk, cleverly designed to look like a 3-D scene. To see it properly, though, you have to stand in exactly the right place. ▶

Brain-Boggling!

These sidewalk illusions work even though you know it has to be a flat picture and, sometimes, you can even still see the lines between the paving stones. That's because once your brain perceives something as 3-D, it's very hard to "unsee" it.

3-D illusion sidewalk art, drawn on a walkway on top of a dam in Poland

GIANT SNAIL ATTACK!

This drawing, by sidewalk artist Julian Beever, is even more cunning. It's partly drawn on a bench to make it look as if a giant snail is climbing up onto it. ▶

How Does It Work?

Sidewalk drawings like this are a popular form of street art around the world. To make a really effective illusion, the artist has to plan what it will show and stretch the drawing out along the ground in exactly the right way. Then, when you look at it from an angle, the way the picture shrinks into the distance makes you see a 3-D image.

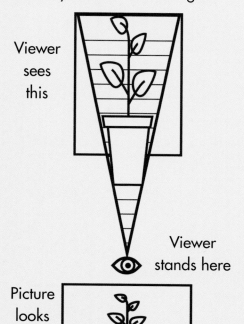

Viewer sees this

Viewer stands here

Picture looks like this

This is what the drawing looks like when you look at it from the viewing point. The humongous, larger-than-human snail seems to be heading up onto the seat to slither all over the person on the bench.

This view from a different angle reveals how the drawing is constructed—in two separate parts that stretch away from the viewer.

WAYS WITH WORDS

You may think you can read perfectly, but think again! The written word can easily fool you.

Can you read the messages in these triangles? Of course you can!

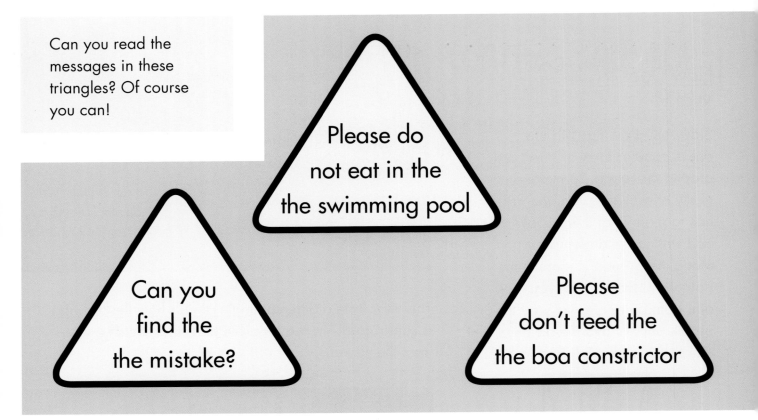

Please do not eat in the the swimming pool

Can you find the the mistake?

Please don't feed the the boa constrictor

Or can you? If the sentences all made perfect sense to you, go back and read them again, more slowly this time.

Many people don't notice that there's a second "the" in each sentence. They simply skip over it and don't see it.

How Does It Work?

When we read something quickly, we don't actually look all that carefully. As with so many other things, the brain takes shortcuts to save time and energy. If a sentence seems simple or familiar, your brain just assumes that it says what you expect it to.

MUMBO JUMBO

This next example is even more amazing. Try reading it, and see how you do.

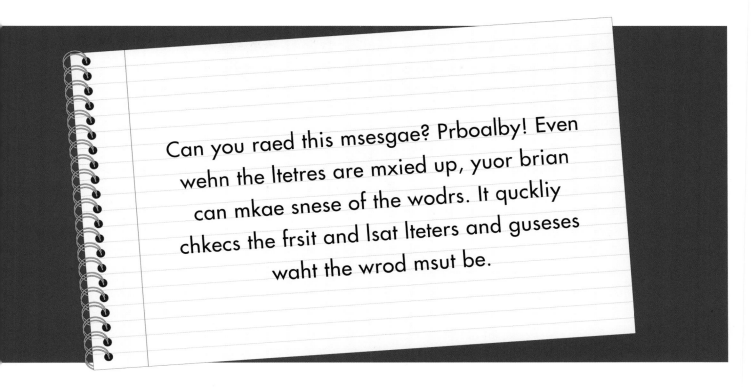

Can you raed this msesgae? Prboalby! Even wehn the ltetres are mxied up, yuor brian can mkae snese of the wodrs. It quckliy chkecs the frsit and lsat lteters and guseses waht the wrod msut be.

You might think that you read by looking at each word carefully, reading the letters in the right order. After all, that's how you learned to read! But your brain has other ideas. It doesn't bother checking each letter—in fact, if it did, you wouldn't be able to read quickly at all. So it just skips along, making a reasonable guess at each word from just a few clues.

Brain-Boggling!

What do you see here? It's a word, but can you read it?

Once you've seen it, this illusion is easy. But at first, your brain is likely to concentrate on the black shapes, since you're used to seeing dark writing on a lighter background. Look at the spaces in between the black blocks, and the word will soon become clear.

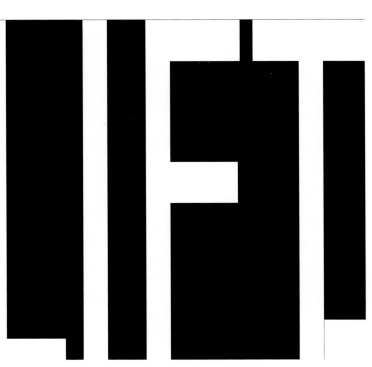

ANIMAL ILLUSIONISTS

Check out these incredible illusions from the world of wildlife.

Humans aren't the only species to make use of optical illusions. Lots of animals do, too—usually to make themselves look more dangerous than they really are, so they can scare away their enemies.

The elephant hawk moth caterpillar's fake snake head

SNAKE IMPRESSION

This could be a snake's head, with big, staring eyes. But it's actually the tail end of a harmless elephant hawk moth caterpillar. If a predator such as a hungry bird saw this sticking out from under a leaf, it would probably stay away. Or if it did decide to bite, it would grab the fake "head," leaving the real head unharmed and giving the caterpillar a better chance to survive.

EYESPOTS

If you saw this huge, golden-ringed eye lurking in the undergrowth, you might think you'd spotted an owl hiding there—or even a big cat, ready to pounce. In fact, it's an eyespot on the wing of an owl butterfly. Because the fake eye is so big, it looks as if it belongs to a much larger and scarier animal.

The owl butterfly's eyespot disguise

SNEAKY OCTOPUS

The ultimate animal illusionist has to be the mimic octopus, which scientists only discovered as recently as 1998. It changes its shape and position to pretend to be a variety of different dangerous animals, including a poisonous lionfish, a stinging jellyfish, and a deadly sea snake.

Here, the mimic octopus sticks two long legs out of the sand, so it looks like a venomous striped sea snake. ▼

GLOSSARY

3-D Three-dimensional, which means having length, width, and depth.

afterimage A leftover impression of an image, caused by the cells in the retina getting used to seeing the same image for a long time.

blind spot A part of the eye where the optic nerve passes through the retina and there are no light-detecting cells.

cells The tiny units that make up living things. Light-detecting cells are found in the retina.

central vision The area in the middle of a person's field of vision, where they see things clearly and in fine detail.

contrasting colors Colors that are opposite to each other, such as blue and orange, red and green, or black and white.

field of vision The area of the outside world that a person can see as they look in a particular direction.

illusion An image that confuses the viewer and makes them see something that is different from reality.

mural A large picture painted on a wall or building, often outdoors. Some murals are also optical illusions.

optical To do with light, and the way our eyes detect it.

optic nerve A bundle of nerve fibers connecting the light-sensing cells in the retina to the part of the brain that makes sense of images.

peripheral vision The area around the edge of a person's field of vision, where things tend to appear blurred and unclear.

perspective The way three-dimensional objects or scenes can be shown on a flat surface, or understood by the brain from the shapes and patterns we see in real life.

retina An area of light-detecting cells at the back of the eyeball that sense patterns of light entering the eye.

trompe l'oeil French for "trick the eye," meaning a flat picture or painting that appears to be a real three-dimensional object or scene.

FURTHER INFORMATION

BOOKS

Gifford, Clive. *Brain Twisters: The Science of Thinking and Feeling.* Brighton, UK: Ivy Press, 2015.

Hanson, Anders, and Elissa Mann. *Cool Optical Illusions: Creative Activities That Make Math & Science Fun for Kids!* Minneapolis, MN: ABDO Publishing Company, 2014.

Sarcone, Gianni A., and Marie-Jo Waeber. *Optical Illusions: An Eye-Popping Extravaganza of Visual Tricks.* Mineola, NY: Dover Publications, 2014.

WEBSITES

kids.niehs.nih.gov/games/riddles/illusions/lots-of-illusions/index.htm
This page has information on lots of illusions.

www.optics4kids.org/illusions
This web page explores 17 optical illusions with a quiz.

Publisher's note to educators and parents: Our editors have carefully reviewed these websites to ensure that they are suitable for students. Many websites change frequently, however, and we cannot guarantee that a site's future contents will continue to meet our high standards of quality and educational value. Be advised that students should be closely supervised whenever they access the Internet.

INDEX